PROFILES OF FLIGHT

SEPECAT JAGUAR

Jaguar GR.1 XZ367/P of 41 Squadron on exercise over Norway. (RAF Coltishall)

PROFILES OF FLIGHT

SEPECAT JAGUAR

TACTICAL SUPPORT AND MARITIME STRIKE FIGHTER

DAVE WINDLE & MARTIN BOWMAN

Pen & Sword
AVIATION

First published in Great Britain in 2010 by
PEN & SWORD AVIATION
An imprint of
Pen & Sword Books Ltd
47 Church Street
Barnsley
South Yorkshire
S70 2AS

ISBN 978 1 84884 237 3

A CIP catalogue record for this book is
available from the British Library

Printed in China through Printworks Int. Ltd

Pen & Sword Books Ltd incorporates the Imprints of
Pen & Sword Aviation, Pen & Sword Family History, Pen & Sword Maritime,
Pen & Sword Military, Wharncliffe Local History, Pen & Sword Select,
Pen & Sword Military Classics, Leo Cooper, Remember When,
Seaforth Publishing and Frontline Publishing

For a complete list of Pen & Sword titles please contact
PEN & SWORD BOOKS LIMITED
47 Church Street, Barnsley, South Yorkshire, S70 2AS, England
E-mail: enquiries@pen-and-sword.co.uk
Website: www.pen-and-sword.co.uk

ACKNOWLEDGEMENTS

I am most grateful to BAe; Squadron Leader David Bagshaw AFC; Mick Jennings MBE; Bernard Noble; Kevin Noble; Gary Parsons; Rolls-Royce and Mike Rondot.

Prototype Jaguar S.07 XW363 carrying a practice bomb carrier (CBLS 100) on the rear station of the undercarriage pylon at Warton in January 1973. (BAe)

On 17 May 1965 the British and French governments agreed to participate in a joint venture to build a supersonic advanced trainer to replace the Folland Gnat in RAF service and the Fouga Magister in the *Armée de l'Air* inventory by 1970. A new supersonic design would also bridge the gap that had opened up since the introduction of more advanced first-line combat aircraft like the Dassault Mirage III in France, while the RAF would need a replacement for the Hawker Hunter by about 1975. The search for a successful combat trainer design with increasingly high strike ambitions not only had to meet an internal French requirement – known as the *École de Combat et d'Appui Tactique* (ECAT), 'tactical combat support trainer' – but it also had to conform to Air Staff Target AST 362 laid down by the Ministry of Defence in London. In effect, the French were looking for a small, relatively simple, cost-effective, subsonic front-line trainer, while the RAF requirement (and to a certain extent, the Royal Navy's) was for a supersonic advanced trainer. France also wanted the aircraft to fulfil an

additional light strike role and be able to operate not only from permanent runways but also from unprepared grass strips. In May 1966 the *Société Européenne de Production de l'Avion d'École de Combat et d'Appui Tactique* (SEPECAT), combining Breguet and BAC, was created and registered in France. The nose, fuselage, centre sections and undercarriage were to be made by Breguet, and the wings, tail unit, rear fuselage and engine air-intakes by BAC. These assemblies would then be mated together on identical production lines at BAC's Military Aircraft Division at Warton near Blackpool, Lancashire, and at Colomiers at Toulouse-Blagnac airport in France, where all eight prototypes would be built. The French and British governments stipulated that the powerplant had to be a collaborative effort also, and in 1966 Rolls-Royce/Turboméca Limited was formed to develop an all-new powerplant. The new RT172 engine was named the Adour, a French river, and production would be centred on Derby and Tarnos in France. All the RAF

Two Jaguars of 54 Squadron during refuelling with Vulcan XH560. (via Dave Bagshaw)

Jaguars of 41 Squadron in formation, with the one nearest the camera taking on fuel from a tanker. (via Dave Bagshaw)

Jaguars would be powered by the Mk 102, and the powerplant was introduced for the eleventh French Jaguar onwards.

Britain and France initially agreed to each procure 150 aircraft, the *Armée de l'Air* receiving seventy-five single-seat 'A' (*appui*, support) strike versions and seventy-five two-seat 'E' (*école*, school) trainers, while the MoD requirement was solely for 150 'B' (British) trainers. Even so, the RAF still desired a much more sophisticated aircraft with supersonic performance and a far superior avionics fit than was required by the *Armée de l'Air*. In 1965 the aircraft received the official name 'Jaguar', and the MoD order for 150 trainers was raised to 200 aircraft by amending the MU to ninety 'S' (strike) examples and 110 'B' trainers. In early 1967 the French requirement was also increased to 200 aircraft, with forty of these being a new 'M' *(maritime)* single-seat strike/reconnaissance version to meet a carrier-based requirement for the *Aéronavale* (*Aéronautique Navale*, or French Navy Aviation) and ten two-seat trainers. In October 1970, with the RAF having been forced to reconsider its requirement, the order was reduced to 165 single-seat strike versions and thirty-five two-seat trainers. Withal, the latter aircraft were no longer to be used as advanced trainers but purely as operational trainers for *ab initio* pilots destined for

Jaguars of 41 Squadron air-to-air refuelling with a Victor XL231 of 55 Squadron. (via Dave Bagshaw)

Jaguar XZ355 of 41 Squadron on exercise in Norway. (via Dave Bagshaw)

SR-71A Blackbird 64-17962 of Det 4 of the 9th Strategic Reconnaissance Wing cruising at 420 knots at 2,000 feet en route to RAF Mildenhall on 2 May 1985. On either side are Jaguars T.2 XX841/S flown by Squadron Leader John Butler and GR.1 XZ119 flown by Squadron Leader (later Group Captain) Steve Griggs AFC, both of 41 Squadron. This unique formation was photographed by Squadron Leader Mike Rondot, Flight Commander 6 Squadron, flying GR.1 XZ359, using an F95 camera in the Jaguar recce pod. (XZ359 crashed on 13 April 1989 north of Berwick-on-Tweed. Squadron Leader Paul 'PV' Lloyd of 54 Squadron was killed.) On 25 May 1982 Steve Griggs had been forced to eject from a Jaguar thirty-five miles north-east of Brüggen when it was 'shot down' by a Sidewinder missile accidentally fired by a 92 Squadron FGR.2 Phantom. SR-71A 64-17962 is now on display at the Imperial War Museum Duxford, where it is one of the star exhibits in the American Air Museum. (Mike Rondot)

Close-up of a 41 Squadron Jaguar from RAF Coltishall. (RAF Coltishall)

out at the BAC factory at Warton on 18 August 1969 and flew for the first time on 12 October, when Jimmy Dell flew it supersonic at the first attempt. Although outwardly the aircraft differed little from the French prototypes, the avionics fit, together with several other internal changes, made it a different aircraft altogether, and it was the first RAF aircraft to have a head-up display (HUD). XW560 was destroyed in a ground fire at Boscombe Down on 11 August 1972. S-07 XW563, the second British prototype, which undertook RAF navigation and attack system tests and ground handling trials, did

not fly until June 1970. This aircraft later had the Elliott digital inertial navigation and weapon aiming system installed (the first of its kind to be produced in Europe) in the 'chisel nose' which was a distinguishing feature of all RAF Jaguar aircraft, though the LRMTS windows were faired over. B-08 XW566, the first British two-seat aircraft, which was built to evaluate training options and take part in navigation and attack trials, was the final prototype Jaguar, and this was flown on 30 August 1971.

The trials undertaken by the prototypes led to changes and

improvements to the airframe. The short nosewheel door with its unique twin landing-light array was extended to full length, the intake splitter plates were deleted and perforations were added to the airbrakes, while the original 'short tail' was extended on two of the British prototypes to provide additional stability during manoeuvring. Starting with prototype B-08, the original one-piece starboard hinging nosewheel door was split into a three-door unit.

The *Armée de l'Air* was the first to receive the Jaguar production aircraft. E1, the first of forty Jaguar Es, flew on 2 November 1971, and deliveries were completed in early 1976. A1, the first of 160 Jaguar As, flew on 20 April 1972, and the last was handed over on 14 December 1981. The first of the production aircraft for the RAF was XX108, which flew for the first time at Warton on 12 October 1973. The RAF's first production two-seat Jaguar, T.2 XX136, flew on 28 March 1972. The first batch of production aircraft was dispatched to Boscombe Down for type proving before the aircraft was released for RAF service. A total of eight front-line RAF squadrons and an operational conversion unit (OCU) were to be equipped with the Jaguar. On 30 May 1973 XX111 was delivered to the Jaguar Operational Conversion Unit (JOCU) at RAF Lossiemouth in Scotland for ground crew training. The JOCU had been established at Lossiemouth in March 1973. The first single-seat deliveries to the JOCU were XX114 and XX115, which arrived on 13 September 1973. The JOCU had a staff of ten instructors who had initially been trained at BAC Warton and went on to train pilots of 54 Squadron, the first operational Jaguar unit, followed by 6 Squadron and the OCU staff. On 30 September 1974 the JOCU was redesignated 226 OCU, which began life with fourteen GR.1 and eleven T.2 aircraft. Students arrived in large courses of ten to fill places on the eight

operational squadrons, which were based predominantly in West Germany. The OCU's primary role was providing seventy-hour courses to pilots with little air time, and including those straight from flying training. During the time that the OCU was responsible for Jaguar pilot training, no fewer than seventeen Jaguars were lost in accidents. When the Jaguar turned 25 in 1998, the OCU had completed over 118 long courses and 135 short courses, or a total intake of approximately 888 students for flying courses. In addition the OCU trained pilots for Oman, Ecuador, India and Nigeria, as well as many exchange officers who have flown the Jaguar for the RAF during this time. In July 2000 16 (Reserve) Squadron moved south to Coltishall, which made the station the last operating base for the Jaguar in RAF service.

RAF Germany was the largest user of the Jaguar, with four squadrons in the strike role and a fifth in the reconnaissance role. RAF Germany formed part of the 2nd Allied Tactical Air Force (2ATAF), and was responsible for interdiction, battlefield support and reconnaissance. At its peak RAFG operated four squadrons of Jaguars in the strike role and one for reconnaissance after conversion in stages from the Phantom FGR.2. The first of the Jaguar units, 14 Squadron, re-formed at Brüggen on 7 April 1975, and was followed by 17, 31 and 20 Squadrons, all of which were declared combat-ready at Brüggen by 1978, with sixteen aircraft each, including one T.2. With the exception of 20 Squadron, the Jaguar units had previously operated the Phantom in the strike/attack role, 20 Squadron being a former Harrier close air support unit. After operating the Phantom FGR.2, 17 Squadron began converting to the Jaguar as RAF Germany's second Jaguar squadron in June 1975. The Jaguar element formed on 1 September and the last of the Phantoms left in February 1976. No. 31 Squadron began conversion from the Phantom in January 1976, to become the third Jaguar squadron at Brüggen. The last Phantoms were withdrawn on 1 July and the Jaguar element became operational with twelve single-seat GR.1 and a T.2 aircraft. Nos 14, 17, 20 and 31 Squadrons formed the largest operational wing in the RAF, with seventy single-seat Jaguars, which were 'declared' to the Supreme Allied Commander Europe (SACEUR) in the most demanding of all the flying roles – dual-role, strike/attack by day and night. In NATO terminology, 'attack' refers to operations with conventional weapons, whereas 'strike' refers to nuclear operations, the ultimate sanction. Additionally, from 1 October 1976, II Army Co-Operation (AC) Squadron's Jaguars at Laarbruch were tasked with tactical reconnaissance until re-equipment with the Tornado GR1A on 31 December 1987. Unlike the Brüggen Wing, the squadron could be committed to any war in the central region. Its pilots were not qualified for in-flight refuelling, which was not considered a requirement in RAFG, and so for deployments the Jaguars either had to fly in stages or be flown by tanker-qualified pilots from UK-based squadrons. Mainly, the squadron was tasked with pre- and post-strike reconnaissance operation in support of the RAFG strike/attack Jaguar squadrons, and latterly the strike/attack Tornado units at Brüggen and Laarbruch. The secondary role of the squadron was attack, using BL755 cluster-bomb unit (CBU) and iron bombs.

The British-based Jaguar squadrons in 1 Group, RAF Strike Command, formed part of the Allied Commander Europe's 'ACE' Mobile Force in conjunction with the 3rd Division of the British Army, and had to be capable of rapid deployment overseas in times of crisis. They would be joined by additional aircraft and crews from the instructor staff of the Jaguar OCU. No. 54 Squadron had re-formed at Lossiemouth on 29 March 1974 to become the first operational Jaguar unit, with aircraft from the JOCU and others minus the LRMTS nose or RWR fin. On 1 October 1974 the 6 Squadron number-plate was handed over from the Phantoms to the Jaguar squadron which had re-formed at Lossiemouth. On 8 August 1974 54 Squadron moved to RAF Coltishall in Norfolk with seven aircraft, and a borrowed T.2 arrived on 23 December. No. 54 Squadron was declared combat ready on 1 January 1975. No. 6 Squadron followed in November, and 41 (F) Squadron became the third Jaguar squadron in the 'Coltishall Wing' part of 1 Group, Strike Command, when it re-formed at Coltishall on 1 April 1977 with the primary responsibility for tactical reconnaissance. The 'Coltishall Wing' was assigned to the NATO-driven Regional Reinforcement and the Allied Commander Europe's Mobile Force, capable of rapid deployment overseas in times of crisis.

The Jaguar participated in the first NATO exercise between 10 and 14 September 1974 when 54 Squadron took part in Bold Guard, operating from Karup air base in Denmark. Their first Red Flag followed in 1978. Two Jaguars of 54 Squadron crossed the Atlantic on Friday 14 July 1978, to re-create to the day a similar event that had happened thirty years earlier. On that occasion, six Vampire fighters from the same squadron made the first transatlantic crossing by jet-powered aircraft. Two Victor tankers of 57 Squadron also flew the 2,260 miles to Goose Bay, refuelling the Jaguars six times each during the five hours forty-three minutes of the flight.

Meanwhile, in February 1978 41 Squadron became part of

Night shift of GR.1s and T.2s of 16 (R) Squadron, the Jaguar OCU on the line. Nearest aircraft is GR.1 'A' with a black tail and the famous 'Saint' emblem in yellow, signifying the squadron's nickname, the 'Saints', because the unit had been formed at St Omer, France, on 12 February 1915 during the First World War. From 1 November 1991, 16 Squadron was associated with the OCU, and the 'Saint' badge worn by Tornado GR1s at Laarbruch until 11 September 1991 was applied to the fin of the Jaguars in addition to their 226 OCU quiver and torch air intake marking and fin band. On 24 June 1994, 226 OCU became 16 (Reserve) Squadron. (RAF)

A Jaguar with overwing AIM-9L Sidewinders taxiing out at RAF Coltishall. (RAF Coltishall)

SACEUR's Strategic Reserve (Air), and in 1983 was assigned to the Allied Command Europe Mobile Force (AMF), both involving regular deployments to northern Norway, operating from the often snow-covered runway at Bardufoss. To support the recce role the squadron had a reconnaissance intelligence centre (RIC), which was responsible for the processing and interpretation of photographs taken by the aircraft. During the NATO Exercise Arctic Express in 1978, 41 (F) Squadron joined detachments of fighter aircraft from a variety of NATO countries. Six Jaguar GR.1s and a T.2 of 41 (F) Squadron were based at Andoya, and they were employed in a variety of tactical reconnaissance, armed reconnaissance and simulated attack sorties. In 1980 six aircraft of 6 Squadron (and 6 of 20 Squadron) took part in Exercise Maple Flag at RCAF Cold Lake with RCAF and USAF strike aircraft. During the second phase 6 Squadron flew an impressive seventy-five sorties.

In France, meanwhile, the Jaguar A1 flew for the first time on 20 April 1972, and a total of 160 A models were delivered to the *Armée de l'Air* by 14 December 1981. The aircraft had less sophisticated avionics than its RAF GR.1 counterpart because of its intended role as a battlefield support/stand-off aircraft role. Beginning in February 1977 with airframe A81, Jaguar As received a Thomson/CSF CILAS TAV-38 laser rangefinder in an undernose blister fairing, and the window for the Omera 40 panoramic camera was moved to the rear of the fairing. (Eventually this was fitted or retrofitted to all A models.) The laser rangefinder, which had been developed for the Jaguar M, was also retrofitted to a small number of earlier aircraft. It had an air-to-ground range in clear conditions of 6.3 miles and was accurate to 16 feet. A131 to A160 were modified to carry the Thomson-CSF/Martin-Marietta ATLIS I and later ATLIS II targeting pod, designed to be used in conjunction with the Aérospatiale AS.30L laser-guided missile or for the stand-off/self-designation of laser-guided bombs. (ATLIS allows the aircraft to launch the missile and break away while the laser pod continues to designate the locked-in target for the missile.) From aircraft A81 the Jaguar As were fitted with a TAV-38 rangefinder under the nose.

The Jaguar E1 first flew on 14 December 1981, and a total of forty

Jaguars of 54, 6 and 41 Squadrons at Coltishall in January 2001. The nearest aircraft is XZ394/GN of 54 Squadron. Behind are XX637/EE, XZ396/EM and XZ372/ED of 6 Squadron. (RAF Coltishall)

two-seat Jaguar Es were delivered for basic conversion and combat training. Fitted with only the most basic of flight systems based on a master gyro and Tacan (SEIM 250-1 twin-gyro inertial platform and an ELIDA air data computer), it also had no in-flight refuelling capability. The Jaguar E was armed with two DEFA cannon with 130 rounds of ammunition, whereas the RAF two-seater had none. The E differed principally from the A model in having a lengthened fuselage to 57 feet 8 inches (17.57 m), including the pitot tube and a tandem bubble canopy, the second seat replacing one of the internal fuel cells and being raised 15 inches (38 cm) higher than the front position. From airframe E27 onwards a fixed probe was fitted on the production line in place of the nose pitot/probe.

The first of 200 production Jaguar (S) GR.1 (Ground Attack/Reconnaissance Mark 1) models (XX108) for the RAF flew on 11 October 1972, and the last aircraft was delivered in 1983. From the outset the GR.1 was much more sophisticated and technically advanced than the Jaguar A, the central hub being the Marconi NAVigation and Weapons Aiming Sub-System (NAVWASS). At the time of its introduction this was one of the most comprehensive and accurate computerised digital inertial navigation and attack systems in the world. It was capable of guiding the aircraft to a target for a single-pass attack without having to use a radar system that could be detected by the enemy. It consisted of the Marconi-Elliott Avionics Systems E3R three-gyro inertial platform; a projected map display; a navigation control unit weapon aiming mode selector; a hand controller and air data computer; the Sperry Gyroscope Divisions gyromagnetic compass and a Smiths Industries diffractive-optics head-up display (HUD) which uses a low-light-level TV camera. Also installed was the Marconi-Elliott MCS 92CM computer, which had an 8,912-

GR.1 XX741 refuelling from a TriStar C Mk 1 of 216 Squadron. (RAF)

VC 10 XV103 tanker of 101 Squadron refuelling Jaguars in 1993. (RAF Coltishall)

wordstore machine to receive inputs from fourteen different sources through the interface unit. The pilot would enter waypoint and target co-ordinates into his MCS 92CM before the mission got under way. During flight, heading, velocity and acceleration information provided by NAVWASS was passed to the pilot via the platform electronic unit and the interface unit via the 92CM computer. Also fitted was a horizontal situation indicator; ARJ 23232 radar altimeter; ARI 23205/4 Tacan and a fin-mounted Ferranti ARI-18223 radar homing and warning receiver (RHWR). Early in the production run a Ferranti ARI 23231/3 laser ranger and

marked target seeker (LRMTS) was added, which resulted in the familiar 'chiselled-nose' appearance of the RAF single-seat Jaguars.

A former Jaguar pilot recalls,

Data inputs to the NAVWASS were made via the pilot's hand controller, which was just behind the throttles and operated with the left hand, the most important button being pressed by the left thumb. Having made the mode selection to start the digital display flashing, the thumb button had to be pressed once to display the number 1 and five times to display

Loading up a Jaguar with bombs on the centre-line stores. (RAF)

5 for each digit. Thus to insert a position in latitude and longitude with a total of eleven digits was a laborious task. As a maximum of up to eight waypoints (turning-points) might require insertion, plus the heights and times at these positions, this process took a considerable amount of time and button pressing, even for a practised operator. The hand controller was also used for slewing the weapon-aiming symbology in the HUD onto the target during attacks – a process known as 'ackling'.

The HUD was projected onto a glass screen in front of the pilot so that he still had a fairly unobstructed view ahead; this was a great leap forward, as he no longer needed to look down into the cockpit to check instrument indications. This display was driven by the INS and showed the flight path in pitch and roll, as well as other parameters such as heading, airspeed and altitude. It was particularly useful for flying instrument approaches down a constant 3° glidepath with speed reducing and alpha (angle of attack) increasing for landing, or flying an accurate 5° dive for dive-bombing. Additionally, it had a mode called velocity vector (VV) in which the aircraft symbol actually pointed where the aircraft was going: placing the symbol just above a hilltop and following the indication took the aircraft just over the bill.

Before flight the pilot inserted details of the stores carried on each pylon into the weapon computer by rotating switches in the nosewheel bay. Considerable care was required, as incorrect selection could result in the release of the whole carrier bomb light stores (CBLS) instead of the individual 3 kg

bombs carried on it. Although a few pilots were caught out, I managed to avoid this particular mistake.

As with most computer-controlled equipments, the weapon-aiming system provided several different modes for attacking targets, probably more than most pilots would need to use, and it enabled weapons to be delivered to a very high degree of accuracy. A great deal of information regarding the aircraft's speed, height, attitude and many other parameters was constantly fed into the computer, which then calculated the best aiming solution. A radar altimeter (normally known as the 'Rad alt') gave accurate height above ground for weapon aiming and general flying, while a laser rangefinder in the nose pointed straight ahead to measure the range to the target. However, the pilot still needed to make all the necessary switch selections correctly, and fly the aircraft precisely, if the best results were to be obtained.

The fuel system contained several tanks and was quite complex, as these fed automatically in a set sequence to keep the aircraft's centre of gravity within limits. Unfortunately, the failure indications in the cockpit were just a couple of lights, and it was very easy to diagnose a fault incorrectly and get into serious problems. The advice was therefore to religiously follow the flight reference cards (FRC), usually referred to as flip cards, and land as soon as possible. The Jaguar carried 3,200 kg of fuel in the internal tanks, plus a further 1,900 kg in the two normal drop-tanks. This was very good for such a small aircraft, and typically was sufficient for an hour and a half to one hour forty minutes on a low-level sortie. The aircraft had two Adour engines, with reheat, which were started by a small jet engine. These engines were quite efficient and used a total of 50 kg of fuel per minute at the normal low-level speed of 420 knots.

The Jaguar was legendary for its lack of thrust. The engines produced only 8,000 lb of thrust each in reheat, and 5,000 lb dry (without reheat), on a heavy aircraft with a small wing. Although it weighed only eight tons empty and had a good thrust:weight ratio at minimum fuel, the normal take-off weight for training was 13.5 tons and the maximum weight was 15 tons. To ensure that maximum thrust was available for take-off, the cockpit pressurisation was usually switched off to avoid bleeding power from the engines. In the event of one engine failing just after becoming airborne, the first action was to select maximum dry power or even reheat on the other engine to maintain flying speed; under hot conditions at full load it might also be necessary to jettison external stores. Normally reheat was only selected at 100% rpm, but for the single-engine landing, maximum dry thrust was not quite enough on the approach. However, minimum reheat was too much, so the aircraft had a unique reheat system with part-throttle reheat (PTR), which enabled reheat to be lit from about 85% rpm upwards.

Beginning in 1978, the Jaguar GR.1's original Adour Mk 102 engines were replaced by Mk 104 (RT172-26) engines very similar to the Mk 804 used to power export versions of the Jaguar, which added between ten and fifteen per cent increase in thrust. The engine replacement programme began with the re-engining of all Jaguars in RAF Germany, and Adour 104s were eventually retrofitted to all aircraft, which became GR.1As. Beginning in 1983, the original Elliott MCS 920M system was replaced on eighty-nine Jaguars by the smaller, lighter, more reliable and more accurate Ferranti FIN 1064 inertial navigation system (INAS), NAVWASS II. No. 54 Squadron was the first to receive the NAVWASS II, which can give twenty types of information on the NCU and PMP, showing the aircraft's present position, track and direction to selected waypoints. These are presented to the pilot on his HUD, which, in addition to the 'regular' flight information, also shows angle of attack, vertical speed, time to go and weapons-aiming information. Among other new innovations for the aircraft was the Ferranti total avionics briefing system (TABS), which was a ground computer linked to a digitising map table. By placing the cursor over a point on his map, the pilot could plot his route, and the computer in turn displayed the completed route, annotating any threats and giving error and time-on-target cues. A hard copy printout showing grid references and up to thirty-one targets or turning-points were then downloaded into a Ferranti portable data store (PODS), a 32 kB erasable memory module, or 'brick', that could be inserted into the aircraft computer via an interface. Jaguars were also provided with an increased weapons fit. This consisted of a Westinghouse ALQ-101 jammer pod and a Phimat chaff dispenser mounted on their outer wing pylons, and two Tracor AN/ALE-40 flare dispensers scabbed onto the underside engine access panels, while provision was made to carry the AIM-9G Sidewinder AAM.

Unlike the Jaguar E two-seater operated by the French Air Force the Jaguar T.2 was designed from the outset to have a full

T.2 XX835/FY taxiing out at a snowy dispersal area. (RAF)

GR.1 XZ106 armed with four 1,000 lb bombs on tandem beams below each wing, with AIM-9L Sidewinders above and Phimat and ALQ-101 (V) jammer pod at Muharraq during Operation Granby. (MoD)

from the GR.1A in having an elongated nose section to accommodate separate and divided cockpits for instructor and student in tandem beneath a large bubble canopy. The aft section was raised by fifteen inches to permit better visibility for the instructor. The avionics were identical to the single-seat version, though there was no internal radar warning receiver (RWR) to permit a smoother transition from training to front-line aircraft. Like the GR.1, the original Elliott MCS 92CM system was replaced by the Ferranti FIN 1064 INAS, and the original 102 Adour engines were replaced by 104s, all aircraft being redesignated T.2A. Every T.2 aircraft was fitted with a retractable IFR probe and a single 30 mm Aden cannon.

Overseas sales of the Jaguar were limited, not least because of Dassault's lack of interest, mainly because their Mirage fighters were a more lucrative option. The export version of the Jaguar remained a collaborative effort, but it was BAC that conducted much of the trials work and weapons clearances, using British prototypes at Warton. And the Jaguar International was based closely on the GR.1A, whose proven avionics and weaponry offered better export potential than the much simpler French version. BAC targeted more than thirty countries as potential customers for the Jaguar, but ironically BAC often lost out to the Dassault Mirage F.1. Although there were no European buyers, the Jaguar International was

operational capability. Originally, thirty-five T.2 operational conversion trainers were ordered for the RAF, though this was later supplemented by three additional T.2s, one for trials work with the Institute of Aviation Medicine and two for the Empire Test Pilots School at Boscombe Down. The first T.2 (production B) first flew on 22 March 1973, with the last being delivered in 1983. It differed

successfully sold to four overseas countries. In September 1974, a month after Oman and Ecuador placed orders for twelve Jaguars apiece, the Jaguar International was publicly launched at the Farnborough Air Show. XX108 was fitted out especially for the occasion with a mock-up of the Agave radar nose and a whole host of weapons options. Oman placed an order for ten single-seat Jaguar S(O).1 aircraft and two Jaguar B(0).2 two-seaters for the Sultanate of Oman's Air Force. The first two aircraft (202/G-BEET and 2004/G-BETB) were displayed at the 1977 Paris Air Show, the first deliveries of the aircraft to SOAF beginning in March 1977. All twelve aircraft, which were powered by the Adour Mk 804 engine, were being delivered by spring 1978 to the Middle East state, where they began equipping 8 Squadron at Thumrait. Later, the unit moved to Al Masirah.

In mid-1980 Oman repeated the original order for twelve more Jaguar Internationals to re-equip 20 Squadron at Al Masirah, and these were all delivered by late 1983. (Later the Jaguars returned to Thumrait when ROAF BAe Hawks were stationed at Al Masirah.) These differed from the first batch in that the single seaters had uprated Mk 811-26 engines and the two-seaters Dash-26 series engines. SOAF Jaguars were fitted with the Ferranti LRMTS nose for the strike/attack role and were configured to carry air-to-air missiles for their secondary role of air defence. The first single-seaters were fitted with overwing launchers for the Matra 550 Magic AAMs, while the second-delivery batch had adapted outboard underwing pylons to carry the AIM-9P Sidewinder. When the Tornado F3 replaced the Jaguar in the air-defence role the Jaguar's primary role became close support and strike. As in the case of RAF Jaguars, Oman's surviving fleet of sixteen single-seat

and three two-seat Jaguars received 1996 and 1997 upgrades, and received FIN 1064 nav/attack systems and the GEC Marconi thermal imaging airborne laser designator (TIALD) system. Rolls-Royce is currently engaged in a programme of activity designed to extend operations of the Jaguar in Oman until at least 2010. Thirty-five of the Jaguar's Mk 811 Adours are being put through a mid-life upgrade, which effectively breathes new life into the engine for an additional 1,200 hours. Once the engines have been upgraded at the East Kilbride facility in the UK, they are then shipped to Oman and run in an open-air test facility. Thumrait is the focal point for the Adour engine maintenance. It serves both the Mk 811s and Mk 871s that power the single-seat Mk 203 Hawks used in the air-defence role and the Hawk Mk 103s, which are used for advanced pilot training, one of the roles initially given to the Omani Jaguars.

Ecuador, meanwhile, acquired ten single-seat ES models and two EB two-seat trainers, all of which were delivered to the *Fuerza Aérea Ecuatoriana* (FAE, Ecuadorian Air Force) by October 1977. As with the RAF and SOAF Jaguars, Ecuador also retained the LRMTS nose and the Marconi-Elliott NAVWASS equipment, and the aircraft were fitted with overwing missile launchers for carrying the Matra 550 Magic AAM and powered by Adour Mk 811 engines. Ecuadorian Jaguars no doubt took part in the border wars with neighbouring Peru, which flared up in 1981 (the Paquisha Conflict) and early 1995 (the Condor War, or 'Alto-Canepa' War) until the signing of a peace treaty in October 1998 ended hostilities between the two countries. By mid-1991 only seven single-seaters and one two-seater remained from the original order, and three ex-RAF Jaguars were acquired as replacement aircraft. Today, only four single-seaters remain in service at Base Aérea Militar Taura, near

Guayaquil, with *Escuadrón de Combate 2111 Jaquares*, part of *Ala de Combate 21*.

In July 1983 Nigeria ordered thirteen single-seat 'NS' and five two-seat 'NB' Jaguar Internationals. Deliveries survived a military coup in December 1983, and all the aircraft had arrived by 1985. The Jaguars were soon withdrawn from service as an economy measure.

It is in India that the Jaguar International has realised its sales potential, where 160 aircraft were selected to replace the English Electric Canberra B(I)58 and Hawker Hunter FGA.56A in *Bharatiya Vayu Sena* (Indian Air Force) service. The order resulted in October 1978 after the Jaguar beat off the very best competing designs, including the Mikoyan-Gurevich MiG-23 Flogger, the Sukhoi Su-20 Fitter and the Dassault Mirage F.l, to emerge the winner of the Deep Penetration Strike Aircraft (DPSA) competition. The successful design had to be capable of low-level penetration and hit targets 300 miles inside hostile territory. Equally importantly, the aircraft had to be available off the shelf, and the bulk of the order had to be produced under licence in India. With an export deal worth £1,000 million, BAe reached agreement with the MoD to supply an initial batch of eighteen Jaguars (sixteen GR.ls and two T.2s) loaned from RAF stock. A further forty Jaguars (thirty-five Jaguar International IS single-seaters and five IT two-seaters) would be built at Warton, equipped with the overwing pylons for Matra Magic AAMs, uprated Mk 811 engines and the BAe reconnaissance pod, and the remaining 120 would be constructed by Hindustan Aeronautics Ltd (HAL) in Bangalore. Despite political infighting in India and more than one attempt by the French government and Dassault to overturn the decision, the deal was honoured, and all the aircraft were eventually delivered to the IAF.

In February 1979 the first four of the twelve IAF officers selected to fly the Jaguar joined Course 29 at 226 OCU RAF Lossiemouth to convert to the type. The first of the ex-RAF 'interim' aircraft left for India in July, where they joined 14 Squadron at Ambala and replaced Hunter FGA.56As. In the summer of 1981, 5 Squadron (The 'Tuskers') at Agra became the second Canberra unit to re-equip with the Jaguar when it re-formed at Ambala, initially with a small nucleus of officers and men drawn from 14 Squadron. The 'Tuskers' were the first unit to receive Jaguars built specifically to the IAF's standard of preparation, which included uprated Adour 804E engines with 27% more combat thrust than the original Adour 102s. Besides the strike role common to all Jaguar units, the 'Tuskers' also assumed a reconnaissance role, initially using BAe-supplied pods. They later standardised on Vinten pods. The 'interim' Jaguars were returned to the UK as promised, after the initial Indian-built production aircraft were issued to 5 and 14 Squadrons at Ambala in mid-1981. The first batch of forty new aircraft powered by the Adour Mk 804 were delivered to India between 5 March 1981 and 6 November 1982. All were fitted with the NAVWASS, which eventually would be replaced by the indigenous display attack and ranging inertial navigation (DARIN) developed at the Aircraft & Systems Testing Establishment in India. The next forty-five aircraft (including ten ITs) were assembled in India from kits supplied by SEPECAT, and were powered by the more powerful Adour Mk 811 engine and equipped with the DARIN system as standard. The first Indian-assembled Jaguar (JS136) flew on 31 March 1982. That summer the first HAL-built Jaguars were issued

Jaguar GR.1 'FM' in a HAS during an exercise in Norway. (RAF Coltishall)

GR.3As XZ103/FP and 'FT' of 41 Squadron with a BAe recce pod and a cluster-bomb unit respectively. For many years the squadron flew with the BAe recce pod that used enough F95 wet-film cameras to provide 180-degree coverage. The 'barge', as it was affectionately known, served with distinction in many theatres, including the 1991 Gulf War and regular visits to Norway. The result of the BAe pod's ageing and the occurrence of more modern technology saw the development of the Jaguar replacement recce pod, or JRRP. This later became the joint reconnaissance pod (JRP) as the new pod was introduced to operational service in the summer of 2000. The JRP featured a smaller housing, making it easier for the Jaguar to carry. It contains either two electro-optical line scanning cameras and a Vigil infra-red line scanner (IRLS) for low-level, or a single EO camera in a swivelling nose for medium-level, work. The IRLS also provided the aircraft with a night recce capability. The JRP has proved so successful that not only was it used operationally on the Jaguar but also on Tornado GR4 and Harrier GR.7 aircraft – although without the same degree of integration and user-friendly simplicity. (RAF)

to 27 Squadron (The 'Flaming Arrows') at Bangalore, where they replaced the unit's Hunter FGA.56As. In October 1986 16 Squadron (The 'Cobras') at Gorakhpur converted to the Jaguar from the Canberra. By now the Jaguar in IAF service was known officially as the *Shamsher* (a Persian word whose literal translation is 'Sword of Justice'). In July 1988 5 Squadron participated in Operation *Pawan*, the Indian Peace-Keeping Force operation in Sri Lanka. In the early days of the operation the Tuskers flew long-range reconnaissance missions, launching from bases well inside peninsular India, overflying Jaffna and then returning to India, often at night. The squadron was on alert to carry out strike missions as well, particularly during the withdrawal of the IPKF, but was stood down without having to use its weapons in anger.

The next batch of Jaguars built in India were thirty-one single-seaters. Included in the last batches were eight Jaguar International IM maritime strike aircraft, which differ from the IS in having nose-mounted Thomson-CSF Agave radar and the capability to operate the BAe Sea Eagle anti-shipping missile. The first of these aircraft flew in 1985 and were delivered to 6 (The 'Dragons') Squadron at Poona (now Pune) near Bombay (now Mumbai), one of the IM aircraft having been lost during development trials, during 1986–93, replacing the unit's Canberras. In 1998 fifteen additional Jaguar IS aircraft were ordered, but these were cancelled a year later. In 1993 this order was revived and is believed to have included four more IM versions. All fifteen aircraft had entered service by the end of 1999. A further seventeen Jaguar ITs were delivered from 2002.

In April 2006 it was announced that Hindustan would build twenty more two-seat training versions of the Jaguar. Jaguar production in India continued until 2007, and the type will remain in service beyond 2010. There is a need to replace the Sea Eagle anti-shipping missile. The majority of strike Jaguars have received phased upgrades, which has included replacing the NAVWASS on the BAe-built aircraft and DARIN on the HAL aircraft with a new system, including an inertial navigation system-ring laser gyro with embedded global positioning system (GPS) receiver. The BAe aircraft have also been fitted with the MIL-STD 1553B databus unit for conformity with HAL-built aircraft. A digital map generator developed by HAL at Korwa reads onto a new head-down display (HDD). A centralised threat-warning system, including a new Indian-built radar warning receiver, has also been incorporated. The upgraded Jaguar first flew in 2002, with the first aircraft being delivered to 5 Squadron late in 2002. The Rafael Litening laser target designation pod will be adopted for widespread use by the fleet.

In June 1994 ten Jaguar GR.lAs and two T.2As were given a laser designation ability that could be employed quickly, especially in Bosnia. Ferranti (later GEC Ferranti) had been involved since 1973 in the development of a laser designator to enable an aircraft to direct laser-guided bombs (LGBs) onto the target. This culminated in the production of the thermal imaging airborne laser designator (TIALD) pod, which had been under flight development on a Buccaneer at RAE Farnborough since early 1988. To permit day-and-night operation under varying weather conditions, TIALD was equipped with thermal imaging and a TV camera, which were mounted in a pod carried beneath the aircraft. The designator was integrated into the aircraft's navigation and attack (nav/attack) system to enable it to be directed and controlled, and the thermal or visual images were recorded by the infra-red recce recorder in the aircraft. Before TIALD, the RAF's ability to use LGBs depended on designation of the target by a manually controlled laser marker. This was operated either from a ground-based designator, as was used in the Falklands conflict, or from the air; in the latter case, the marker equipment was fitted to a Buccaneer and controlled by the navigator. Although it was employed successfully by Tornado GR1A aircraft during the Gulf War, there were several limitations to this system. The main one was that the navigator needed to see the target visually, thus limiting its use to good weather by day. Additionally, it could not be integrated with a modern nav/attack system. Also, having located the target, the navigator had to track it visually – not easy in turbulence or if the aircraft was taking evasive action.

TIALD had been trialled for the Tornado aboard Jaguar T.2A XX833 'Night Cat', one of a number of aircraft used by the DRA (which in April 1995 became the Defence Evaluation and Research Agency) for passive night-attack studies. XX833 had originally been delivered to RAE Farnborough on 8 April 1988 for laser modifications. These included a new HUD, the MIL-STD 1553B databus and a new HDD. The aircraft then flew with an underwing GEC-Marconi podded airborne targeting low-altitude thermal imaging and cueing (ATLANTIC) Type 1010 FLIR system to test procedures and monitor the aircraft's other arrangements, such as presenting an image onto the HUD and HDD. The Night Cat later flew with an 'A-Model' TIALD pod, which was subsequently removed and rushed to the Gulf for urgent operation in Operation Granby.

In the event UOR 41/94 was achieved mainly by using and modifying the equipment already being trialled for production, and the TIALD pod was fully integrated into the Jaguar's avionics systems and harmonised with the INS, being mounted on the aircraft centre-line station, where fewer obstructions obscure the field of view. As well as the interface for the TIALD equipment (using a MIL-STD 1553B databus), it was inside the cockpit that the new toys were most obvious to those familiar with the 'old machine'. Improved navigation equipment and cockpit displays, including a Marconi FD 4500 A4 wide-angle HUD, were installed. The 1:1 ratio wide-angle head-up display and associated up-front controller replaced the peculiar 5:1 geared version of old, and with the new HUD came the capability to display, a multitude of real-time information. To enable TIALD operation in a single-seat cockpit a 'hands on throttle and stick' (HOTAS) arrangement was created by using stick tops from Tornado F2s and hand controllers from scrapped Harrier GR.3s, HOTAS functions reducing time spent 'head in cockpit' dealing with navigation-button-pressing and weapon-aiming facilities. Out went the microfilm-fed moving map display, and in its place an HDD consisting of a Marconi PMD with GEC symbol and digital map generators from the Tornado GR4 upgrade programme was fitted. This unit, which later became known as the multi-purpose colour display (MPCD) could display a digitally generated map or the image seen through the newly acquired TIALD pod by displaying TV/IR imagery in video-style format. The FIN 1064C taken from Tornado and Harrier stocks improved navigational accuracy and allowed automatic target acquisition by the TIALD tracker. To record TIALD imagery Vinten dual video recorders were installed. In its 'designator' role the Jaguar also carried a Phimat AN/ALQ-101 (V)-10 jammer pod and two 264-gallon (1,200-litre) fuel tanks. The rear warning radar was

GR.1B XX729/EL of 6 Squadron with a GEC Marconi thermal imaging airborne laser designator (TIALD) system on the centre-line. Behind is XZ362/GC of 54 Squadron with a 1,000 lb (454 kg) laser-guided bomb on the centre-line and a 41 Squadron Jaguar carrying a 1,000 lb free-fall bomb. Both are armed with overwing-mounted AIM-9L Sidewinders. (Rick Brewell)

uprated to 'Sky Guardian' 200-15 standard. While it was designed for daylight operations, during the mid-1990s trials were undertaken to make the Jaguar fleet compatible with night-vision goggles (NVGs). All twelve TIALD aircraft were delivered to Coltishall within twelve months, the last arriving in spring 1997. Modifications to cockpit lighting and capability to use the exterior station-keeping lights were subsequently fitted to the majority of

the fleet. T.2A XX835 and T.2A XX146 were modified to serve as airborne TIALD instructional aircraft which in time of war were to serve as laser designator aircraft.

Following on from the success of the original GR.1B and T.2B programme, a further two-stage upgrade was introduced to bring the remainder of the Jaguar fleet up to the same standard. As far as the Jaguar was concerned, the MoD had only to pay for the upgrade

Jaguar T.2 'X' of 41 Squadron taxiing during an overseas detatchment. (RAF)

work, and not the design, making it cheaper to add capability to the Jaguar than to any other front-line aircraft, to the extent that the Jaguar's out-of-service date was delayed twice. The programmes took on added importance when delays in the Eurofighter Typhoon programme pushed back the retirement date of the Jaguars from operational service, so that they would have to remain viable for a longer period than originally thought. The terms 'Jaguar 96' – the first phase of the upgrade programme – and 'Jaguar 97' – bringing all the aircraft to a common standard – were applied as these were the scheduled dates for their service entry. These modifications included the full list of Granby modifications and the modifications introduced on the GR.1B/T.2B. Once all these modifications had been incorporated, the designation of the Jaguar became

Jaguars of 41 and 54 Squadron with **Armée de l'Air Mirage** *2000Cs in April 2000. A month later, on 31 May, XX745/GV (nearest the camera) was involved in a mid-air collision with XX832/EZ T.2A of 6 Squadron during a sortie over Scotland, and both diverted into Leuchars, Fife. XX832 suffered only slight damage, but XX745 received severe damage to the underside of the cockpit area and was assessed as CAT 4. Next are XX720/GB and XZ363/FO, which was lost on 26 July 2001 during Exercise Cope Thunder at Eielson AFB, Alaska, during a simulated ground attack. Flight Lieutenant Jason Hayes was killed. Then come XX829/GZ, XZ367/GP (which flew in Operation Granby as 'Debbie', later 'White Rose') and XZ103/FP. (RAF Coltishall)*

Profiles of Flight

GR.3 and T.4. The upgrades changed the Jaguar from a low-level strike and reconnaissance aircraft to a medium-level platform capable of employing precision-guided munitions (PGMs). Much of this change was brought about through the efforts of Wing Commander Pete Birch, the Jaguar Upgrade Project Officer (JUPO). His 'Jaguar 96' standard introduced a databus into the aircraft avionics architecture – a network that connects the aircraft's 'black boxes'. 'Jaguar 97' really furnished this network with up-to-date equipment.

Jaguar 96 used the MIL-STD 1553B databus, making the aircraft compatible with smart weapons, even though the majority of aircraft could not use them, and each was wired for TIALD, if not compatible with the podded system. The wide-angle HUD used on the Jaguar GR.1B was installed. The excellent Ferranti FIN 1064 INAS, which allowed the Jaguar to be operated accurately and reliably at low level, was updated by integrating a GPS receiver and the BASE terrain profile-matching system (TerProm) to give outstanding accuracy and performance with weapon aiming

XZ115 and XZ355/J of 41 Squadron in Arctic scheme camouflage in March 1990. XZ355 was previously one of a batch used by II (AC) Squadron, which disbanded on 31 December 1987 and re-equipped with the Tornado GR1A. (RAF Coltishall)

38

B(0).2 of 20 Squadron of the SOAF (Royal Air Force of Oman) in a HAS at Thumrait. Thirty-five of the Omani Jaguars' Mk 811 Adours were put through a mid-life upgrade, which effectively breathes new life into the engine for an additional 1,200 hours. Once the engines were upgraded at the East Kilbride facility in the UK, they were then shipped to Oman and run in an open-air test facility. (Rolls-Royce)

GR.1 XX122/GA of 54 Squadron with overwing Sidewinders. XX122/GA crashed on 2 April 1982 into the Wash off the Holbeach Range, killing the Norwegian pilot, who had become disorientated in the hazy weather. (RAF Coltishall)

GR.3A 'FM' landing at RAF Coltishall on 14 June 2005. (Author)

built onto one computer card acquired from the C-130J Hercules programme were installed in some of the Jaguar 96 aircraft. On the ground, planning a sortie could now be done on the Jaguar mission planner (JMP), a PC-based system using a similar database to that of TerProm. It allowed pilots to choose very careful routes through known surface-to-air missile threat areas and minimise aircraft exposure in hostile territory. XX738, the first Jaguar 96, which flew

for the first time in January 1996, was delivered to RAF Coltishall in March 1997. Not all Jaguar 96s were of a single standard, some being compatible with TIALD and others with the recce pods, while the rest, depending on the configuration of the aircraft upgraded, could use all of these systems. Full clearance for the Jaguar 96 was gained in February 1998.

The main aim of Jaguar 97 was to give each aircraft the ability to

T.4 XX838/FZ of 41 Squadron taking off from RAF Coltishall on 14 June 2005. (Author)

use TIALD and podded reconnaissance systems and to slave the TIALD system to a GEC Marconi/Honeywell helmet-mounted sighting system (HMSS). For the pilots the HMSS and the data link (IDM) were the key capabilities of the GR.3A, both of which made the Jaguar unique in the RAF. The IDM transmits information between up to eight aircraft and a ground station known as a 'Termite'. A forward air controller (FAC) who moves with ground forces and calls in air strikes can send coded targeting information directly into the Jaguar's navigation system. Not only was this a great improvement in efficiency, but it also means that the FAC transmits far less on the radio and is therefore less vulnerable to enemy direction finding. The IDM also transmits

GR.3A XZ114 taking off from RAF Coltishall on 14 June 2005. This aircraft operated with both 41 and 6 Squadrons and was a Gulf War veteran. (Author)

GR.3As XZ398/FA and 'EH' of 41 Squadron at RAF Coltishall on 29 March 2006. (Author)

present position (PP) data around the network. If he wishes, the pilot will see the position of the other members of his formation on his moving map in the cockpit almost continuously, so the pilots are better placed to look after each other while on a mission.

The HMSS fitted to a standard HISL Alpha lightweight flying-helmet incorporates a tiny projector that projects a varying combination of crosses, circles and squares onto the inside of a pilot's visor, in front of his right eye. This removes the need for the pilot to 'look down' into the cockpit while operating the TIALD pod.

HMSS can also be used in the air-to-air role to point the Sidewinder AAM missile towards an enemy aircraft and also to designate points on the ground. It is this second facility that is especially important to pilots. Most contemporary exercises and operations rely heavily on medium-level close air support (CAS). CAS is the FAC calling air strikes onto enemy positions. If the FAC needs to call in medium-level CAS, he talks the pilot's eyes onto the target by using features on the ground: woods, lakes, railways, road junctions. Once the pilot and FAC are sure that they are talking

GR.3A XX767 of 41 Squadron at RAF Coltishall on 29 March 2006. (Author)

Close-up view of GR.3A XX767 of 41 Squadron at RAF Coltishall on 29 March 2006. (Author)

about the same position, then the FAC can clear the pilot to attack the target – a procedure routinely used in Afghanistan and Iraq. A Jaguar pilot could dispense with much of the talking. Once the FAC has sent a target over the IDM, it would be a matter of seconds before the pilot was looking at the target. Conversely, if a pilot saw something of interest, he could designate it and the aircraft computer would derive a latitude, longitude and height for that position. This target could be sent to another Jaguar, to the FAC or to anyone with an IDM on the network.

Jaguar 97 also had the ability to use the Paveway III laser-guided bomb. Another enhancement was the fitting of the common rail launcher (CRL) on the overwing Sidewinder pylon. In the cockpit the MPCD was replaced by a GEC Marconi portrait format active matrix liquid crystal head-down display (AMLCD) with twenty-eight multi-function soft keys and excellent sunlight glare rejection. The AMLCD is better able to show the digital moving map and TIALD imagery, as well as other flight information, than the MPCD. The Jaguar 97 also has a fully integrated Jaguar mission planner (JMP). The route planned on the JMP is downloaded to the aircraft using a data-transfer cartridge. Multiple routes can be loaded to the cartridge, giving the aircraft navigation system access to well over a thousand way-points. The information can be displayed on the AMLCD showing the track lines, way-points and targets, as well as timing and heading information. The NVG-compatible cockpit includes new filters, electro-luminescent floodlights and replacement panel illumination. The first Jaguar 97 (XZ3990) flew on 4 August 1997, and the type gained its military aircraft release on 14 January 2000. Single-seat Jaguar 97s became GR.3As, and two-seaters T.4As, which did not have the ability to use the HMSS.

The final element of the Jaguar improvement programme was the award of a mid-1998 contract by the Jaguar and Canberra Integrated Project Team (IPT) to upgrade the Adour 104 engines to Mk 106 standard. The earlier engine experienced hotspots in the jet pipe caused by unregulated mixing of air and fuel, which could lead to fire in the engine bays and even the loss of the aircraft. The purpose of the upgrade was to reduce the number of problems per flight hour with the Adour Mk 104 from six to two. (Though increased thrust was not the prime reason for the upgrade, re-engining produced a 5–6% increase in the thrust available to the aircraft, leading to improved airfield performance.) The hotspot problem was particular to the Mk 104, whereas the phenomenon is not as problematical on the Mk 811, which powers the export version of the Jaguar. The Adour Mk 106 is based on the dry section of the Mk 871 used in the Hawk and USN Goshawk, and the Mk 811 afterburner unit is used on the export Jaguars. Compared to the Mk 104, it has a modified fairing to smooth the air/fuel flow in the jet pipe and clamps to restrict the fuel injection in critical areas of the pipe. Although the total number of Jaguars that would use the new engine was not expected to exceed sixty aircraft, 122 engine conversions kit sets were manufactured to cover operational requirements until the end-of-service date, and a number of spare engines, at a cost of £105 million. This figure included four development Adour Mk 106s, which were produced for engine testing and flight trials. BAe Systems at Warton flight-tested the new engine in Jaguar GR.1A XX108 (S1, the first production single-seater for the RAF). Phase 1 trials, involving a Mk 106 in one engine bay and the baseline Mk 104 in the other, began in July 2000 and were followed by a pair of Mk 106s built to slightly differing standards being fitted and flown. Slight problems in the jet pipe were remedied by Rolls-Royce before Phase 2 began in July 2001, when two full production Mk 106 engines were used. Flight testing was completed in November 2001, and EPA.1 (engineering production aircraft 1, GR.3 XZ400) was delivered to RAF Coltishall on 24 January 2002. The last of fifty upgraded single- and two-seat aircraft were returned to service early in 2005.

When Iraq invaded Kuwait on 2 August 1990, and the Saudi Arabian government requested assistance, the RAF's contribution to air power in the Gulf was second only in importance to that of the United States of America. Within forty-eight hours of the Defence Secretary Tom King's announcement that the government was sending large-scale forces to the Gulf in Operation Granby, a squadron of Tornado F3s arrived in Saudi Arabia, and two hours later they flew their first operational sortie. First word of a possible Jaguar GR.1A deployment from RAF Coltishall came on 8 August. Immediately, the Norfolk station began to generate thirteen aircraft and prepare more than 300 personnel for a rapid move to the Middle East, though at this stage the final destination was unknown. Hectic activity followed during the next forty-eight hours, with all Coltishall personnel working extremely hard to prepare the deploying squadron for possible Gulf operations. The three resident Jaguar squadrons had a rapid deployment role within NATO, and as such were well practised in the art of swift reaction, and the station's previous hard training was now paying off. Operational requirements dictated that the detachment was to be made up of more pilots and ground crew than a normal Jaguar squadron, and so the decision was made not to send a single numbered squadron but to make up the unit with personnel from the whole wing at Coltishall. Additional support was provided by crews from 226 OCU at RAF Lossiemouth.

All thirteen Jaguars (a dozen were destined for the Gulf, while the thirteenth – XX766 – would remain at Coltishall as a spare) were given an overwash of 'desert sand' ARTF (alkaline removable temporary finish), reportedly designed for low-level operations. Each aircraft carried a Westinghouse AN/ALQ-101 (V) jamming

The last of the Jaguars after a downpour at Coltishall on 1 April 2006. (Author)

'contacts' with Boeing C-135FR tankers of the *93ème Escadre* at Riyadh. The Jaguars began returning to France on 5 March.

On 18 January Wing Commander William Pixton and his four-ship element flew the first RAF Jaguar bombing mission, a Republican Guard unit west of the Kuwait–Iraq border. Each aircraft carried overwing AIM-9Ls with auxiliary fuel tanks being carried on the inner wing stations. This left only the centre-line hard-point available for the carriage of two 1,000 lb free-fall bombs.

(Within days, the configuration was changed, the underwing fuel tanks being replaced by tandem beams and the centre-line station devoted to the carriage of fuel, so that up to four 1,000 lb bombs could be carried in tandem pairs under each wing. Fusing options varied depending on the target, with airburst, impact and delayed action being employed.) Wing Commander Pixton was to recall,

Whether we hit anything when we dropped our bombs, I'll never know. What I do know is that my first encounter with

55

GR.3A XZ112/GW (left) and XZ117/FB (right) after a downpour at Coltishall on 1 April 2006. (Author)

the enemy frightened me almost senseless. I will never forget looking at that yellow globe and wondering what it was, and I will always be amazed by how long it took me to register that it was AAA and by the strength of reaction once realisation dawned. I've been a combat-ready Jaguar pilot for years – but today, for the first time, I understand what it means.

Better weather on 19 January resulted in the first full day's operations for the RAF Jaguars, and twenty sorties involving four separate missions were scheduled. The first was launched at 0425 hours with an eight-ship attack on SA-2 SAM and AAA sites. All eight Jaguars returned safely at around 0845 hours, as did a second four-ship-formation mission to Iraq. The third formation of four Jaguars took off at 0910 hours and attacked more AAA batteries before returning safely. The fourth and final four-ship mission, after a change of aircraft to the ones used earlier in the day, took off at

1255 hours to attack more AAA batteries. All returned safely at 1405 hours.

It was soon decided that medium-level missions would offer better protection from the threat of AAA and shoulder-launched SAMs on combat missions. As well as friendly fighters there was suppression of enemy air defences (SEAD) provided by USAF EF-111A Ravens jamming Iraqi radars, while F-4G Wild Weasels were ready to engage any SAM site that showed signs of launching. There was also a constant commentary on SAM/MA threats and enemy fighter activity by E-3 Sentry AWACS and EC-130E Airborne Battlefield Command and Control Centre (ABCCC). With the decision to change to medium level, the retard tails on the 1,000 lb (454 kg) bombs were replaced by free-fall fins. The Hunting BL755 cluster-bomb unit (CBU), which can only be delivered effectively from low level, was replaced by the Bristol Aerospace (Canada) LAU-5003B/A pod containing nineteen CRV-7 2.75 in. (7 cm) high-velocity rocket projectiles. The CRV-7, which underwent proving trials in the UK in late 1990, and was cleared for operational use, was used from the outset. The pod and nineteen rocket projectiles, which can be fired singly or in a 'ripple', has a total weight of just 530 lb (240 kg), and aircraft carried two of the pods per mission. Because of its high speed of around Mach 4, CRV-7 is accurate over ranges of 6,000 metres, but a hurried integration with the Jaguar's weapons-aiming computer resulted in inaccurate deliveries, and it was temporarily withdrawn from the inventory. (Ferranti provided rewritten software within two weeks, and CRV-7 was soon reinstated.) As an interim measure the American CBU-87 Rockeye II cluster-bomb, which, unlike BL755, could be released from the new operating height above 10,000 feet,

was introduced with effect from 29 January, although it was too long for more than one to be carried on a twin-carrier beam. Most bombing missions were flown thus, the weapons fused for air burst, impact or delayed action. Paveway II laser-guided bombs were also trialled for use by the Jaguar, but they were not carried during the war.

Throughout the short conflict the primary role assigned to the RAF Jaguars was battlefield air interdiction (BAI). One or two missions were made against targets in Iraq, but before Desert Sabre and the start of the ground war, the Jaguars' main operational axis was the area south of Kuwait City, which was very well defended by AAA. Targets included SAM and AM sites, SY-1 Silkworm SSM batteries, coastal and inland fixed and mobile artillery pieces, Astros multiple rocket launchers, armoured columns, barracks, storage facilities and at least one airfield. Once Desert Sabre began and the Allied advance turned into a rout of the enemy forces, JagDet's main area of operations soon moved up to the area north of the Kuwaiti capital, and from thenceforward missions were mainly directed against the Iraqi Republican Guard. Kuwait and Iraq were divided into 'kill zones', and primary and secondary targeting instructions were passed from the Coalition headquarters in Riyadh on the day before the mission was to be flown, so that planning and preparation could begin. Then the mission data were fed into the Ferranti FIN1064 digital nav/attack system. The pilots on standby would receive a final intelligence update from the ground liaison officer (GLO) and a five–ten-minute brief on the target area (with emphasis on the defences) before it was time to walk.

The majority of the twenty-two pilots in JagDet were given attack tasks, with twenty pilots being organised into 'constituted fours'. Two of the Jaguars were normally configured for reconnaissance operations, and their primary objective was to take pre-strike pictures of target areas as a supplement to satellite imagery in the planning process. On reconnaissance missions one of the Jaguars carried a Vinten LOROP pod, and the other a standard BAe pod with an F126 survey camera in place of its vertical linescanner. This was because, while the LOROP imagery offered remarkable resolution, its narrow field of view and lack of a data matrix made results difficult to determine, and so comparison with F126 imagery was made to enable reconnaissance interpretation centre (RIC) personnel to achieve satisfactory results. The aircraft completed thirty-one sorties in twenty-one separate reconnaissance missions. Squadron Leader Dave Bagshaw AFC and Flight Lieutenant Pete Livesey, the 'recce specialists', almost invariably operated as a pair, although Baggers flew some solo reconnaissance sorties, usually latching onto a four-ship for extra protection. During the Gulf War five of his twenty-four missions were bombing operations.

Generally, aircrew flew a four-days-on/one-day-off routine, with the flight schedule being arranged to permit a forty-eight-hour interval between each duty period. Thus, following a day off a constituted four would return to action on the afternoon wave, flying as the second element of an eight-aircraft group. On the next day, they would have responsibility for planning and leading the afternoon wave, again of eight aircraft. After this, they would operate as the second element on the following morning's early raid before ending up as the lead element on the morning of the fourth duty day. With this mission completed, they would then have a forty-eight-hour break before resuming the cycle. A typical flying day required JagDet to mount two eight-aircraft attack waves, for a total of sixteen sorties. After each mission the pilots would go to debrief, which often lasted longer than the mission itself, since it invariably included electronic warfare analysis, study of HUD videos, discussion of RWR indications and notification of visual identifications of SAM and MA sites to the GLO. This level of activity was sustained for most of the campaign, apart from weather disruptions or the very occasional technical problem.

On 26 January the Jaguars made a highly successful dawn attack on an SY-1 Silkworm coastal anti-ship missile battery in Kuwait, as part of preparations for an amphibious landing. Although the much-publicised potential assault by the US Marine Corps was a deception, it would have gone ahead had the Coalition's ground thrust deep into Iraq misfired. On 29 January Jaguars again attacked Silkworm sites, using the CBU-87 cluster-bombs for the first time. On 30 January, when the Jaguars destroyed an artillery battery north of, and command bunker south of, Kuwait, Wing Commander William Pixton AFC and Flight Lieutenant Peter 'Frog' Tholen destroyed a 1,120-ton Polnochmy-C-class landing-craft. On 31 January the Jaguars attacked artillery in southern Kuwait. On 1 February two Jaguars diverted from another mission to attack a ZSU-23/4 flak vehicle in south-east Kuwait with cluster-bombs. On 3 February the Jaguars raided ammunition dumps south of Kuwait City and dropped 1,000 lb (454 kg) air-burst bombs successfully on six Iraqi artillery emplacements on Faylakah Island, ten miles off the Kuwaiti coast. On 5 February, with Iraq's navy virtually destroyed, support combat air patrol (SuCAP) and the associated combat search and rescue (CSAR) operations ceased after forty-eight sorties (twenty-three missions). Mostly these missions, which

GR.3A XZ112/GW (left) and XZ117/FB (right) after a downpour at Coltishall on 1 April 2006. (Author)

typically were of three to four hours' duration and required air-to-air refuellings, involved pairs of Jaguars armed with bombs, rockets and cannon, which maintained a CAP while they orbited waiting for 'trade'. Bombing of the Republican Guard intensified during the second week of February, while on the 12th the campaign against Iraqi communications was supported by a mission against a

pontoon bridge constructed to replace one knocked down by LGBs a few days before. The final phase of the Jaguar's war brought individual artillery pieces into the target lists, an early success being the destruction of five Astros multi-ramp rocket launchers on 13 February. Once the land war began on 24 February, Jaguars

GR.3A XX396 '1973–1998 25 Years' at RAF Coltishall on 1 April 2006. (Author)

operated exclusively north of Kuwait City for the remaining three days of war.

During Operation Desert Storm the RAF Jaguars flew forty-eight SuCAP/CSAR sorties on twenty-three missions, thirty-one reconnaissance sorties on twenty-one missions and 538 BAI sorties on 114 missions, for a total of 617 sorties on 158 missions. They dropped 750 1,000 lb (454 kg) bombs, 385 CBU-87 Rockeye IIs and eight BL755 CBUs, and fired 608 CRV-7 2.75 in. rockets from thirty-two LAU-5003 pods. About 9,600 rounds of 30 mm ammunition

were expended and three AIM-9L Sidewinders (including one that was accidentally launched) were fired at enemy targets. Total combat hours amounted to 920 hours 15 minutes.

Further cuts in French Air Force Jaguar numbers were made following the Gulf War, and sixty Jaguar A and Es were allocated to the three units of the *7ème Escadre* at St Dizier, with the remainder being placed in storage or sent to ground training units. Jaguars participated in Operation Aconit, as part of the UN's joint Operation Provide Comfort over Iraq, policing the no-fly zones.

The sun sets on the Jaguar at RAF Coltishall on 1 April 2006. (Author)

Saddam Hussein had begun attacks against the Kurdish population in the mountainous regions in the north of Iraq bordering Iran, Turkey and Syria, which resulted in massive refugee problems for those three countries. The UN responded by establishing a safe haven and security zone for the Kurdish people. An area of Iraq above 36° N was also designated an air exclusion zone to Saddam Hussein's air force. To ensure compliance with the UN resolutions, a Coalition task force comprising the USA, UK and France was formed to patrol the area, primarily to discourage Iraq from infringement but also to respond in the event of any flagrant disregard of the UN edict. Turkey agreed to join the Coalition force for Operation Warden, as it

This was followed by Operation *Crécerelle* over Bosnia, which began in April 1993 as part of the *Armée de l'Air* contribution to enforce UN Resolution 781 and the air exclusion zone. The Jaguars' main role was to provide an all-round bombing capability, as well as reconnaissance over Bosnia-Herzegovina. In June 1994 the French formed part of the UN humanitarian effort in the beleaguered African country of Rwanda, when Jaguar As and ten Mirage F1CR-200s, supported by C-135F tankers, were based at Kisangani airbase, near Goma, to provide reconnaissance and air support to ground troops.

After the cease-fire in the Gulf War the RAF Jaguars returned home to Coltishall to a heroes' welcome, but soon another detachment was being prepared to fly back to the Gulf region.

was called, and operations were to be conducted from the Turkish Air Force Base at Incirlik. The USAF provided the air defence and fighter-bomber role, shared with the Turkish Air Force, while the UK and France provided tactical photographic and reconnaissance cover, as the USAF did not have this component in Europe. The UK committed eight Jaguar GR.1A aircraft, and France a similar number of Mirage F1CR-200s, both dedicated to observe and record Iraqi military activity within the exclusion zones. The Jaguar GR.1As were selected as the most suitable aircraft as their BAe and Vinten VICON LOROP pods recorded their imagery on film, unlike the Tornado GR1As, which used video cameras.

The UK commitment was formed during August 1991, with eight Jaguars drawn from all three squadrons at Coltishall, and painted in the now familiar desert pink scheme. Although 41 Squadron was the only Jaguar unit dedicated to photographic reconnaissance, both 6 and 54 Squadron pilots had been trained to undertake this role, as each squadron provided aircrew and ground crew on a two-monthly rotation. The first four aircraft departed Coltishall on 4 September, followed by the remaining aircraft five days later. No. 41 Reconnaissance Intelligence Centre (RIC), plus support personnel and equipment, was flown out to Turkey by C-130 Hercules aircraft. In addition, the VC 10 tankers of 101 Squadron, which supported the initial deployment of the Jaguars in their non-stop flight, were to remain in theatre to provide air-to-air refuelling cover for the duration of Operation Warden.

The Jaguars, generally operating in pairs, one armed with CBUs, a second configured for reconnaissance, were required to regularly overfly all known military sites and photograph the activities to provide constantly updated intelligence. Targets included Iraqi troop concentrations, air defence sites, military airfields (at least five were located within the no-fly zone), railway termini, barracks and vehicle parking areas. All of the targets were located within Iraqi territory and were potentially hostile. Therefore the Jaguars carried defence packages consisting of overwing-mounted AIM-9L Sidewinder missiles, 30 mm Aden cannon and an electronic countermeasures suite that included the Phimat chaff/flare dispenser and an ALQ-101 jamming pod on underwing hard-points. Periodically the recce pod was replaced by 1,000 lb bombs to demonstrate to the Iraqis that the Coalition was ready and willing to respond with force if needed. The Mirage F1CR-200s invariably performed their recce task in the mornings, while the Jaguars flew slots later in the day. The location of each target to be photographed

was carefully plotted on a large map to determine its exact position. The number of aircraft required to perform the mission was also determined by the number of subjects that needed to be photographed, although the normal sortie rate saw the Jaguars working in pairs, with up to six aircraft flying per day. Missions usually lasted two hours and were flown with support packages provided by USAF F-16s or F-15s, defence-suppression F-4G Phantoms and ECM-jamming EF-111 'Spark Varks' or USN EA-6B Prowlers and tanker support.

The personnel of 41 Squadron were the first to deploy on Operation Warden during the late summer of 1991, and were the last of Coltishall's squadrons to participate prior to being replaced by the Harrier force in April 1993. Two months earlier, on 22 February, twelve Jaguars of 6 Squadron departed Coltishall for the Italian Air Force base at Gioia del Colle in southern Italy, when Coalition forces were once again tasked to support an international operation. Deny Flight, for which the UK's participation was known as Operation Grapple, was designed help maintain the United Nations Protection Force (UNPROFOR) in Bosnia-Herzegovina in the former Yugoslavia. From thenceforth 6 Squadron shared the manning of the detachment with 54 and 41 Squadrons. The Jaguars at Gioia were representative of the Coltishall wing, although with the application of a new colour scheme (ARTE light grey, designed for medium-level operations), the only method of determining squadron ownership of the aircraft was by the two-letter code on the tail and nosewheel door. The aircraft were fitted and prepared to Operation Granby standard, which included overwing AIM-9L Sidewinder launchers, Tracor flare dispensers, Phimat chaff dispenser and AN/ALQ-101 ECM pod, and 'tweaked' engines, the

Four Jaguars of 41 (R) Squadron at RAF Coningsby fly over RAF Coltishall in salute at the end of the closure ceremony on 30 November 2006 which marked the end of the line for this famous Battle of Britain fighter station. (Author)

were tasked to attack a Red Force convoy a hundred miles (160 km) from base. Flying at high transonic speeds at very low level, the Jaguars arrived unopposed and undetected at the target, much to the surprise of the Red Force aggressors. The following year 54 Squadron's Jaguars returned to Red Flag and 'shot down' two USAF F-15 Eagles!

In Germany the RAF remained on full alert and exercised regularly on the continent and further afield to remain at the forefront of the NATO deterrent. Defending NATO's northern flank was a prime function of the Jaguars of the Coltishall wing, and annual deployments were regularly made to the Royal Norwegian Air Force Base at Bardufoss, in northern Norway, 120 miles inside the Arctic Circle. All the aircraft that took part were normally given the standard Arctic colour scheme, consisting of an 'overwash' of white ARTE while the normal full-colour squadron markings were retained. No. 41 (F) Squadron was the declared Arctic specialist in the Jaguar wing, although 6 and 54 Squadrons also regularly

deployed to the inhospitable snowy wastes as part of their rapid-deployment capability. With the ending of the Cold War, Britain's forces, and in particular the RAF, were able to renew old traditions and exercise with former WarPac air force units in Poland, Bulgaria and Romania.

Following the announcement that RAF Coltishall was to close as part of the 2004 Defence Review, the first tangible evidence of the draw-down was witnessed on Friday 11 March 2005, when 16 ® Squadron and 54 (F) Squadron disbanded at the Norfolk station, following 170 years' combined service. On 1 April 2006, 41 (F) Squadron handed over the squadron numberplate to the Fast Jet and Weapons Operational Evaluation Unit at RAF Coningsby, and the squadron's illustrious history continued as 41 (R) Squadron. On the same day, 6 Squadron moved back to RAF Coningsby, to continue flying the Jaguar until October 2007, when the aircraft was replaced by the Typhoon.

Worldwide Operators
Bharatiya Vayu Sena (Indian Air Force)

Units	Date	Base	Role
5 'Tuskers' Squadron	8/81–current	Ambala	Strike/reconnaissance
6 'Dragons' Squadron	1981–current	Pune	Maritime strike
14 'Bulls' Squadron	9/80–current	Ambala	Strike
16 'Black Cobras' Squadron	10/86–current	Gorakhpur	Strike
27 'Flaming Arrows' Squadron	1/85–current	Gorakhpur	Strike
Aircraft & Systems Testing Establishment	–	Bangalore	Testing

Fuerza Aerea Ecuatoriana (Ecuadorian Air Force)

Units	Date	Base	Role
Escuadron de Combate 2111 'Aguilas' ('Eagles') now *Jaguares*	1977–	Aérea Militar Taura	Strike

Nigerian Air Force

Jaguar International SN	705-717
Jaguar International BN	700-704

Armée de l'Air (French Air Force)

Unit	Date Formed	Disbanded	Role	Base
Escadron de Chasse 3/3 Ardennes	10/3/77	29/3/87	SEAD	Nancy
Escadron de Chasse 1/7 Provence	24/5/73	7/2005	Strike	Saint-Dizier
Escadron de Chasse 2/7 Argonne	1/5/74	30/6/01	OCU	Saint-Dizier
Escadron de Chasse 3/7 Languedoc	14/3/74	30/6/01	Strike	Saint-Dizier
Escadron de Chasse 4/7 Limousin	1/4/80	31/7/89	Strike	Istres
Escadron de Chasse 1/11 Roussillon	1/3/76	31/7/94	Strike	Toul
Escadron de Chasse 2/11 Vosges	3/11/76	31/7/96	ECM/SEAD	Toul
Escadron de Chasse 3/11 Corse	7/2/75	31/7/97	Strike	Toul
Escadron de Chasse 4/11 Jura	1/1/79	30/6/92	Strike/recce	Bordeaux
Centre d'Instruction Tactique 339	5/9/88	7/2001	Combat training	Luxeuil
Escadron de Chasse 5/330 Côte d'Argent	–	–	Test	

(OCU – operational conversion unit, SEAD – suppression of enemy air defences)

Al Quwwat Al Jawwiya Al Malakiya As Omaniya **(Royal Air Force of Oman)**

Serials

Jaguar International DB	201, 203, 213, 214
Jaguar International OS	204-212/215-224
Jaguar GR.1	226
Jaguar GR.1 (Interim)	225
Jaguar T.2 (Interim)	200

Units	Dates	Base
6 Squadron	3/77–current	Thumrait
20 Squadron	1983–current	Thumrait

RAF Jaguar Units

	From	To	Role
II (AC) Squadron	February 1976	December 1988	Tactical recce RAFG
6 Squadron	October 1974	to Eurofighter 2007	OAS
14 (F) Squadron	7 April 1975	14 October 1985	OAS RAFG
16 Squadron	November 1991	13 March 2005	OCU
17 Squadron	June 1975	1 March 1985	OAS RAFG
20 Squadron	1 March 1977	24 June 1984	OAS RAFG
31 Squadron	1 July 1976	31 October 1984	OAS RAFG
41 Squadron	April 1976	1 April 2006	Target recce
54 (F) Squadron	March 1974	13 March 2005	OAS
226 OCU	October 1974	to 16 Squadron	OCU

(OAS – offensive air support, OCU – operational conversion unit)

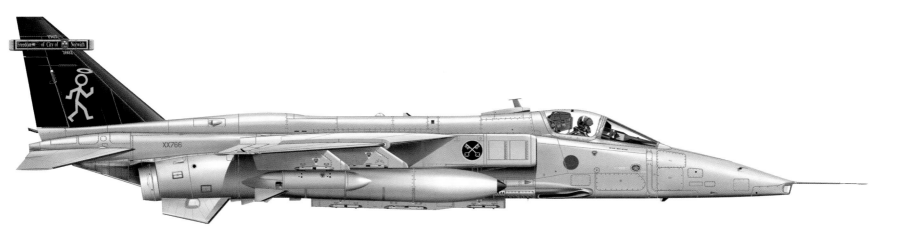

Jaguar GR.Mk 3A XX766 of **No.16 (Reserve) Squadron**
Freedom of the City of Norwich 1967 - 2002

Jaguar T.Mk 4 XX835 'EX' of No.6 Squadron
Retirement of the Jaguar and squadron disbandment 30th April 2007

Jaguar GR.Mk 1A XX962 'X' of **No.6 Squadron**
Gulf War 1991

Jaguar GR.Mk 3A XZ103 of **No.41 Squadron**
2005 display aircraft

Jaguar GR.Mk 3A XZ103 of No.41 Squadron
Disbandment scheme 1st April 2006

Jaguar GR.Mk 3A XZ112 'GA' of No.54 Squadron
Disbandment scheme 1st April 2005

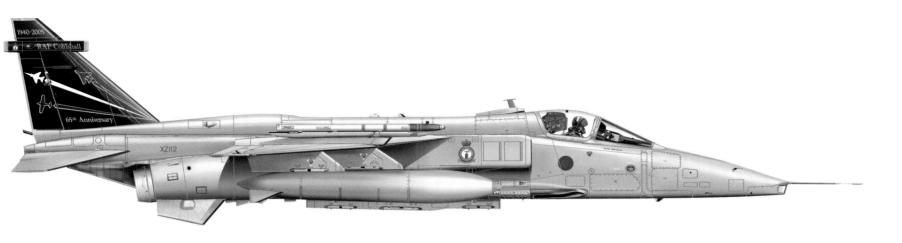

Jaguar GR.Mk 3A XZ112 of No.6 Squadron
Coltishall 65th anniversary 1940 - 2005

Jaguar GR.Mk 3A XZ364 of **No.54 Squadron**
Coltishall 60th anniversary 1940 - 2000

Jaguar GR.Mk 1A XZ396 of **No.6 Squadron**
25 Years of Jaguar operations 1973 - 1998

Jaguar T.Mk 2A ZB615 of the **Royal Aircraft Establishment,
Defence Test & Evaluation Organisation**
and **Empire Test Pilots School**
The last Jaguar built for UK service. Aircraft retired from flying in 2005